# Welcome

May your love grow stronger each and every passing year. This journal will serve as a record of how, when and where you met your spouse. It can serve as a testimonial for both of you to record the feelings, ups and downs that you go through during your first year of marriage.

# This book belongs to

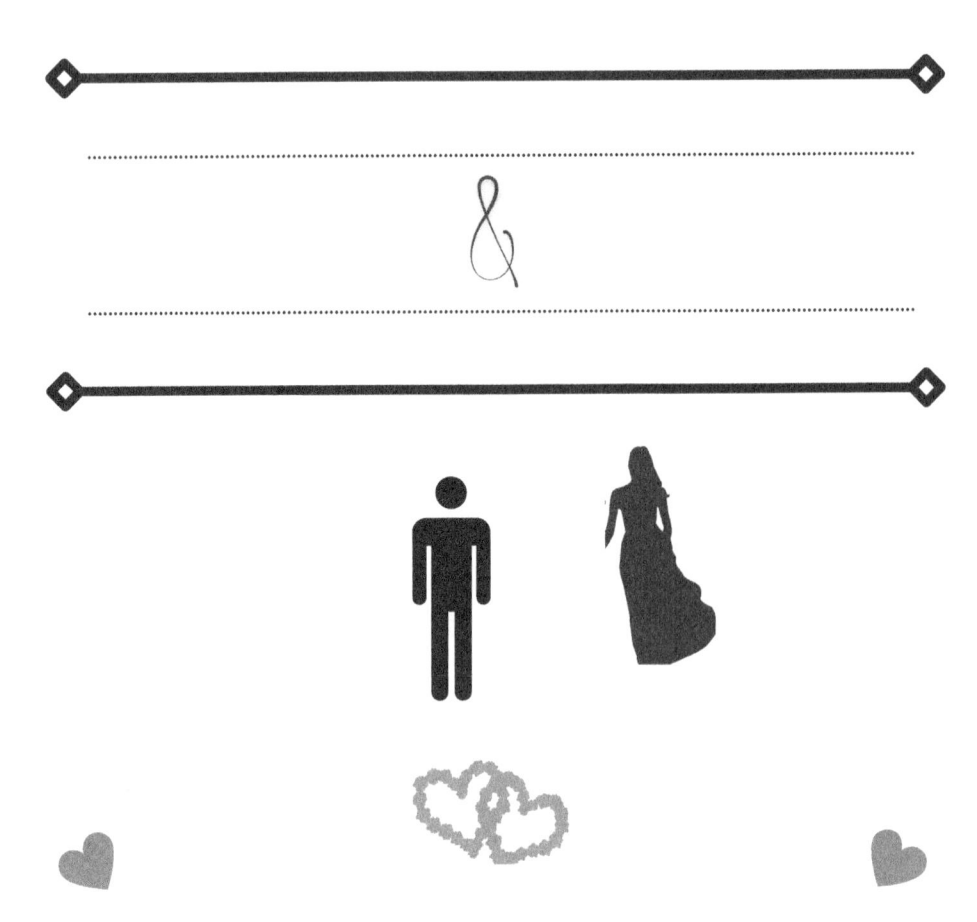

&

# Where we First met?

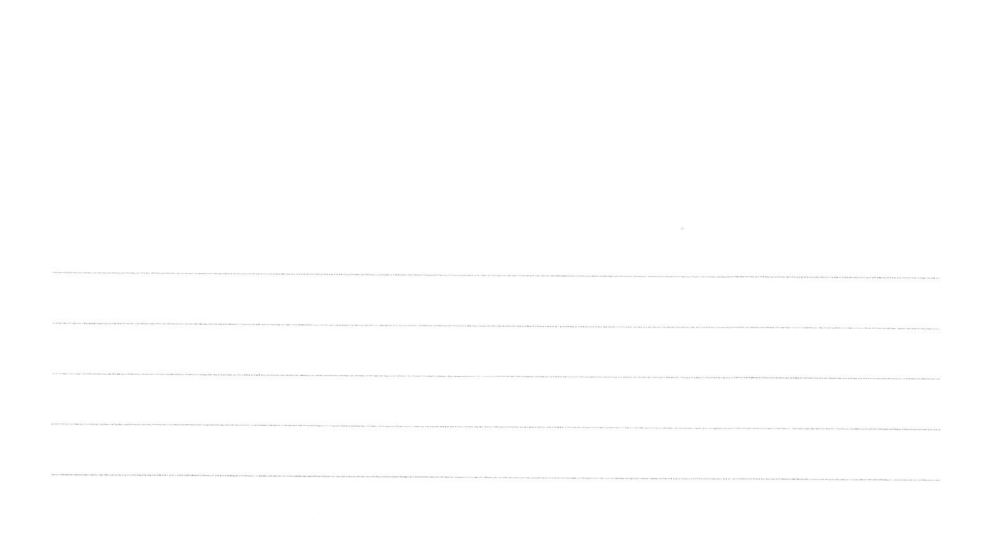

# When and how we met?

# Who made The First move?

# Who said I love you First?

# Your spouse in one word

# What is your spouse birthday?

# What did your partner wear on your first date?

# What movie did you first watch together?

# Where did you go on your first date?

# When did you know that they were 'the one'?

# When and where was your First kiss?

# Who is a better kisser?

# Who is the tidiest?

# Who is the Funniest?

## Who is their celebrity crush?

## Which one of you is a better driver?

## Who does the most cooking?

# Who is the best cook?

# Who does the most cleaning?

# What's your spouse's favorite TV show?

You are in a party & the DJ is playing your Favorite song. What song is it?

# How many dates did it take before you kissed?

## How long had you been dating when you became engaged?

## How many guests did you invite to the wedding?

## What adjective best describes your spouse on your wedding day?

# Is your spouse more like their mom or their dad?

# How does your partner tell you that they're in the mood?

# Who of their friends is your spouse most similar to? how?

# Does your spouse have a catch phrase? What is it?

# What's a story your spouse tells to every new group of friends?

## If your spouse could spend $500 on anything, how would they spend it?

# What 5 adjectives would your spouse use to describe themselves?

# What does your spouse talk about the most?

# What's your spouse's Favorite joke to tell?

# What adjective would your spouse use to describe you?

# Your spouse has $100 to spend for you. What do they buy?

# What word would your spouse use to describe your family?

# What emoji best represents your spouse? Circle it.

30

# What was the most recent gift that you got from your spouse?

IF you could live anywhere in the world, where would it be? Where would your spouse like to live if they had a choice?

# Where would your spouse choose to go on a dream vacation?

# If you planned your dream vacation, where would you go and what would you do?

# How many kids do you want? How many does your partner want?

## Out of the two of you, who is more decisive?

# What was the last thing you two argued about?

_____
_____
_____
_____
_____

# What is your spouse's Favorite thing to cook?

# Which one of you is the first to fall asleep at night?

## If the two of you went to visit a pet shelter together, would your partner head to the dogs or the cats first?

## If the two of you were on a date, which one of you would be the most likely to look at your phone during the main event of the date?

# Who will your spouse say is the more romantic one in your relationship?

## If your partner were to describe you as a superhero, who would it be?

# When it comes to Food, does your lover prefer Mexican, Italian, Chinese, or American?

## Does your lover prefer juice, coffee, soda, or something else with their breakfast?

# Would your partner say that you're the type of person who likes to try new things or stick to their guns?

## What are two things you have in your house that your partner could never live without?

## When you plan to go out for dinner, what two restaurants would not be on the list of choices?

# What is your spouse's Favorite thing to cook?

# Complete the sentence

I really wish my spouse would

at home.

We are complete opposites
when it comes to

One thing we will never, ever
agree on is

One thing my spouse would never do is

I knew I had found the love of my life when they

When my partner wakes up in the morning they are likely to find my \_\_\_\_\_ on her \_\_\_\_\_

Not many people know it but my spouse is really good at

Not many people know it but my spouse is really good at

If I were to dye my hair he would like it to be

My partner can fix _____
but when it comes to fixing
_____ , he needs a little
professional help

# Thank you

We appreciate you choosing this book, and we hope you enjoyed answering the questions.
Feel free to leave a review on Amazon. Your feedback is most welcome.

2022 ©

Amen Press

Printed in Great Britain
by Amazon